This Is a Let's-Read-and-Find-Out-Science Book®

How Do Apples Grow?

by Betsy Maestro

illustrated by Giulio Maestro

■ HarperCollins*Publishers*

The illustrations in this book were done in
pencil and then colored with watercolors.

The *Let's-Read-and-Find-Out Science Book* series was originated by Dr. Franklyn M. Branley, Astronomer Emeritus and former Chairman of the American Museum-Hayden Planetarium, and was formerly co-edited by him and Dr. Roma Gans, Professor Emeritus of Childhood Education, Teachers College, Columbia University. For a complete catalog of Let's-Read-and-Find-Out Science Books, write to HarperCollins Children's Books, 10 East 53rd Street, New York, NY 10022.

Library of Congress Cataloging-in-Publication Data
Maestro, Betsy.
    How do apples grow? / by Betsy Maestro ; illustrated by Giulio Maestro.
        p.   cm. — (Let's-read-and-find-out science book)
    Summary: Describes the life cycle of an apple from its initial appearance as a spring bud to that point in time when it becomes a fully ripe fruit.
    ISBN 0-06-020055-3. — ISBN 0-06-020056-1 (lib. bdg.)
    1. Plants—Reproduction—Juvenile literature. 2. Apple—Reproduction—Juvenile literature. 3. Flowers—Juvenile literature. 4. Fruit—Juvenile literature. 5. Seeds—Juvenile literature. [1. Apple. 2. Plants—Development.] I. Maestro, Giulio, ill. II. Title. III. Series.
QK827.M33 1992   91-9468
582'.0166—dc20   CIP
                                                               AC

When you bite into a juicy apple, you're eating part of a flower. Fruit comes from flowers.

In winter, an apple tree is bare. It's hard to imagine
it covered with flowers or fruit.

4

But even in the cold and snow, tiny leaf buds and flower buds are waiting to open.

Inside each leaf bud are tiny, curled-up leaves.
Inside each flower bud are all the parts of an apple
flower.

buds

Apple flowers are pink and white, and sweet to
smell. And each flower is the beginning of an apple.

When spring comes, there are more hours of sunlight. The days are longer and warmer. The leaf buds open. Tiny green leaves appear on each twig. When the apple tree is covered with leaves, the flower buds begin to open.

Up close, you can see bunches of small pink-and-white flowers at the end of each twig.

Each flower can become an apple. But all the right things must happen first. An apple flower has many parts, and each has a special job to do.

apple flower buds

sepals

Around the outside are the sepals. They form a little cup to protect the rest of the flower. As the flower blossoms, the sepals open too.

The pretty, colored petals and sweet, flowery smell bring many insects and birds to the apple tree. These animal helpers are needed for flowers to make fruit.

flower
petals

sepals
opening

stamens

Inside each flower are the male and female parts that make a new apple grow. The male parts are called stamens. Each flower has many stamens. If you look inside an apple flower, you can see all the stamens sticking up in a circle.

At the top of each stamen, pollen is made. Pollen is a yellow powder. Each flower has thousands of pollen grains. Each grain of pollen holds male cells.

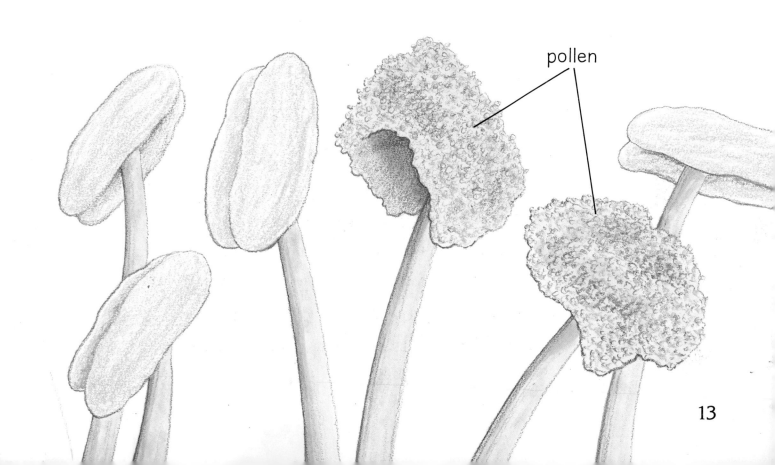

pollen

The female part of the flower is called a pistil. You can see some of the pistil right at the center of the flower. The pistil has tiny tubes with sticky tops.

At the bottom of the flower, out of sight, these tiny tubes meet. The place where the tubes meet is the ovary. The ovary is the part of the pistil that holds the female cells. The ovary will become the inside core of the apple.

pistil

ovary

15

An apple can grow when the male cells join with the female cells—when the flower is fertilized. The male cells from the pollen have to reach the female cells in the ovary.

This sounds easy, but it's not. The apple flower can be fertilized only by pollen from a different apple tree. Since apple trees can't move, they can't carry the pollen themselves. They need helpers for this job.

Bees are some of the apple trees' best helpers. Bees are attracted to the colorful petals of the flowers. They like the smell of the sweet flower juice, the nectar.

Bees fly from tree to tree, collecting nectar. They will use the nectar to make honey. As the bees gather nectar, pollen grains stick to their bodies. When they land on the flowers of other apple trees, some of this pollen falls off.

The grains of pollen land on the sticky tops of the pistil's tubes. The male cells in the pollen grains travel down these tiny tubes. At the bottom, they reach the ovary. Here, the male cells join with the female cells. The flower is fertilized.

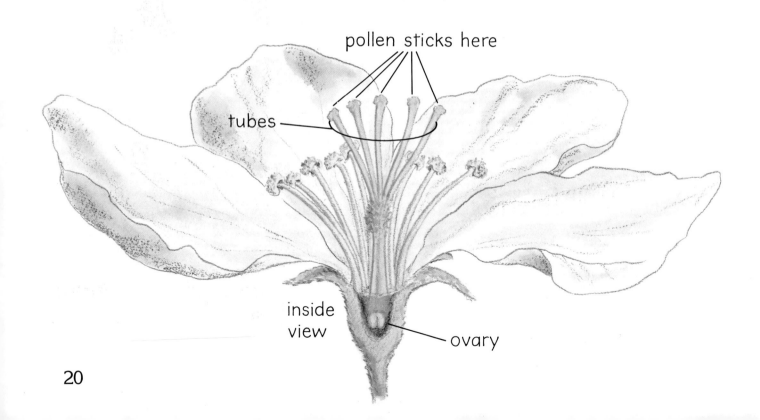

pollen sticks here

tubes

inside view

ovary

Now the petals fall to the ground. The petals are no longer needed. They have done their job.

The flower has been fertilized. Now an apple will begin to grow. It will grow right at the spot where the flower meets the stem.

As the fertilized ovary grows bigger, it forms the apple's core, which holds the seeds. They will be well protected here. Around the ovary, the rest of the apple is swelling too. This is the white, fleshy part that you can eat.

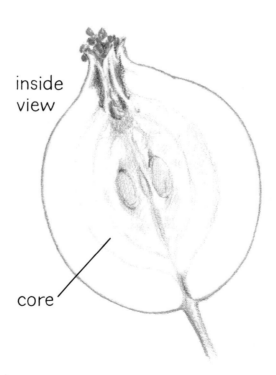

inside
view

core

Look at the bottom of a ripe apple. You can see
bits of the dried sepals left from the flower.

When the apple is cut open, you can see the seeds. Look carefully, and you'll see five little compartments or sections. There may be as many as ten seeds inside your apple.

The seeds are the fertilized female cells. Apple seeds can grow into new apple trees.

The apple tree must feed the growing apples. By using sunlight, water and air, the leaves make a special kind of sugar. This sugar feeds the fruit. It takes about fifty leaves to make the sugar for one apple.

All summer long, the apples grow bigger and riper.

When fall arrives, the apples are almost ripe. During the last few weeks, the apples can feed themselves. They make their own sugar now. The sugar makes the apples sweet.

Red Delicious

McIntosh

Golden Delicious   Granny Smith

Sunlight helps the leaves and the apples to make food. It also helps to change the skin color of some apples. Different kinds of apples have different skin colors. Some turn red, and others turn yellow. Some varieties of apples stay green even when they are ripe.

When the apples are ripe, it is time for picking. If no one picks the apples, they will fall to the ground. Animals will eat some of them, and may carry the apple seeds to other places. Some of these seeds will grow into new apple trees.

Some of the apples may just rot on the ground. After a while, they will become part of the soil. They will help to feed the tree.

As fall ends, the trees lose their leaves. New buds are already forming. They will be next year's apples. For now, the apple tree's work is over. For you, it's time for the best part. It's apple-eating time!